On the Wings of an Albatross

An A-Z

of

Australian and New Zealand Birds.

Elizabeth Gordon-Werner

Did you know that birds have hollow bones which help them fly ?

A for Albatross

Albatrosses can fly very
long distances. They have
tendons that lock the
wings so they can
keep them open
without any effort
and soar on the
wind instead
of flapping.

The Albatross has the widest
wingspan of any bird of up to
3.5 meters or 11 feet 6 inches.
So if an albatross wanted to
visit you, it should close
its wings and waddle
through your door.

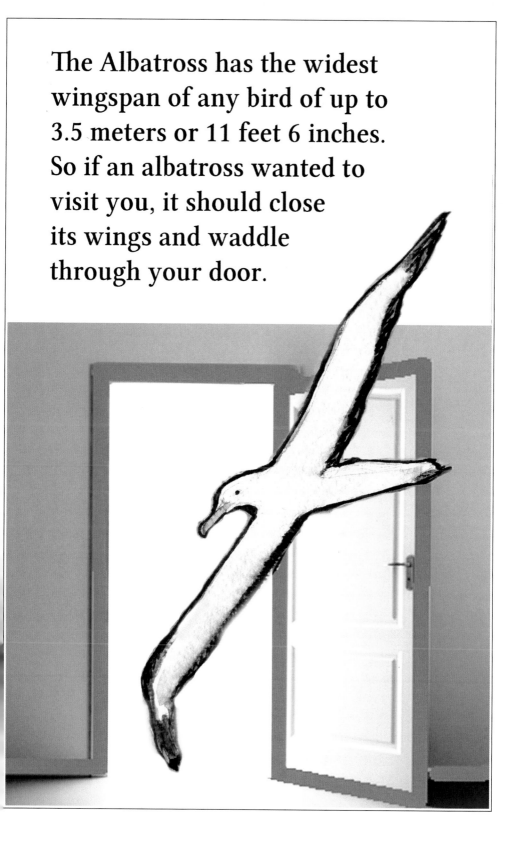

B for *Brolga*

The Brolga is
well known in
Australia for its mating dance.

The birds jump and stretch and
bow and bob their heads up
and down.

The Brolga Christmas song:
Out on the plains the brolgas are dancing
Lifting their feet like warhorses prancing
Up to the sun the woodlarks go winging
Faint in the dawn light echoes their singing
Orana! Orana! Orana to Christmas Day.

The Brolga is a big bird
but its wingspan is less than
the Albatross.

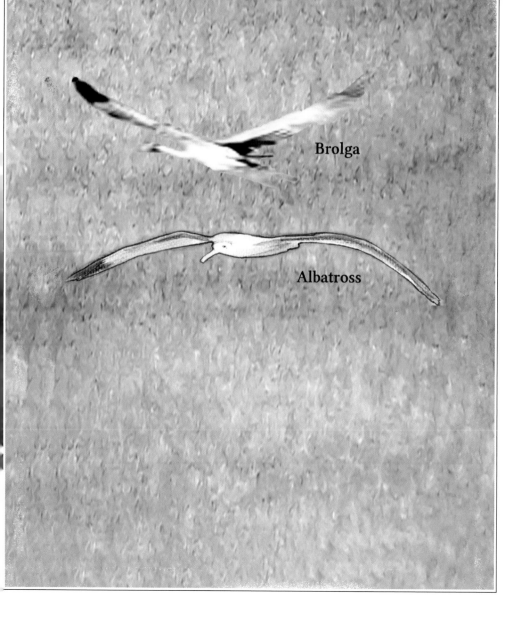

Brolga

Albatross

C for Currawong

Currawongs are big black birds that look a bit like magpies or crows but they have a hook at the end of their sharp beaks.

In trees they fly as if they are falling between the branches.

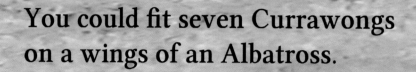

You could fit seven Currawongs
on a wings of an Albatross.

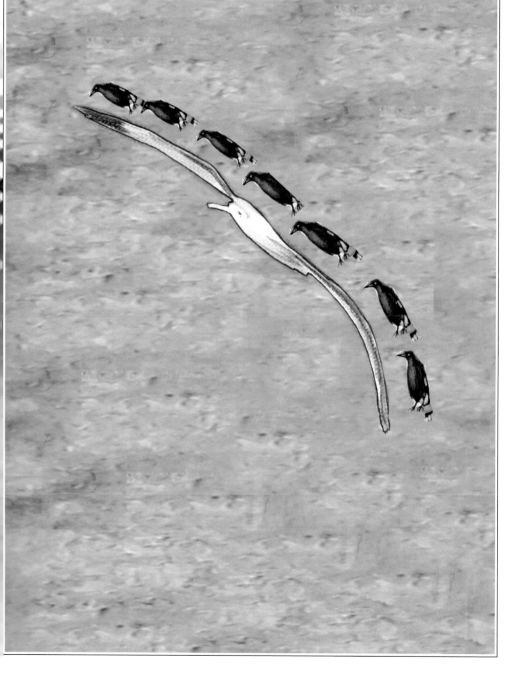

D for Duck

The paradise duck is a pretty bird.
The male is mostly black and
the female has a white head
with a chestnut body.
They live in pairs, grazing on
grass and weeds.

Five and a half ducks fit
along the wings of an Albatross.

(But where is the half duck?)

E for Emperor Penguin

Emperor penguins
live in big groups
in Antarctica. Each
penguin has a
different call so
it is easy for
them to find
their partners
and their chicks.

The chicks have
different whistles to
beg for food and to call
their parents.

Emperor Penguins are 120cm from beak to tail so three penguins could lie along the wings of an Albatross.

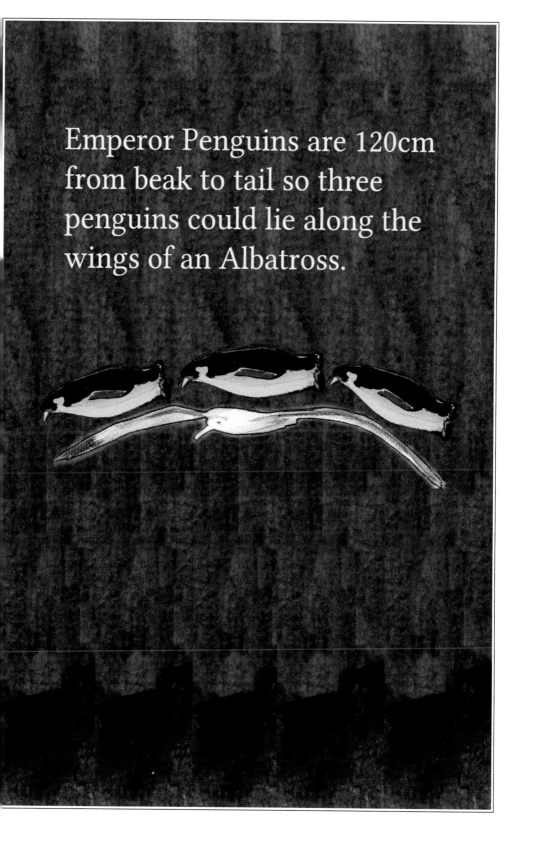

F for Fantail

Fantails are friendly little birds that eat insects. They are never still, flitting among the trees looking for flying insects. They like being with people who disturb insects when they walk or dig in the garden.

Seventeen Fantails would fit on the wings of an Albatross.

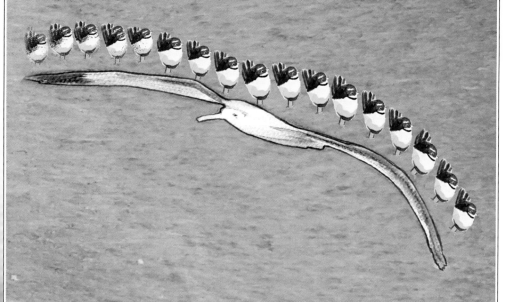

G for Galah

Galahs are intelligent,
playful and talkative.
They live almost
everywhere in
Australia.

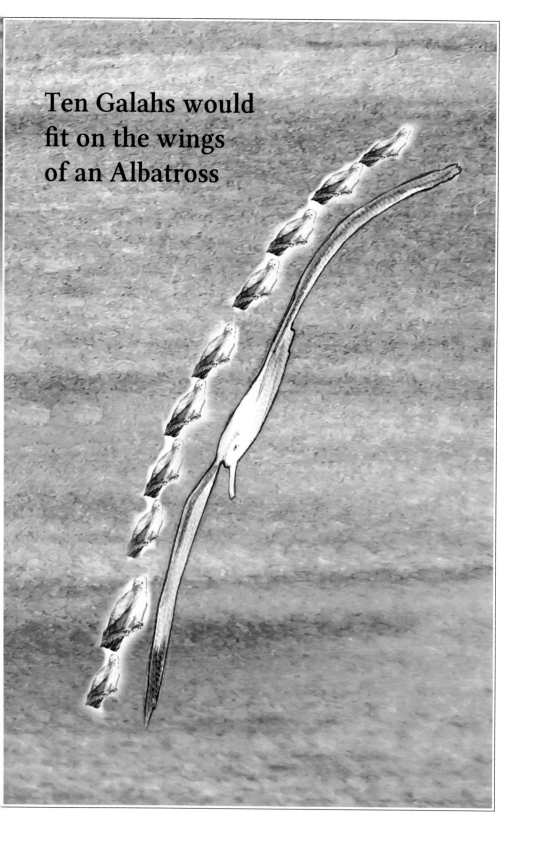

Ten Galahs would
fit on the wings
of an Albatross

H for Hahawai

The Hakawai
is a mythical
bird to the
Maori people.
It is black
yellow and
green with a
tuft of red
feathers on
its head.

The Hakawai is said to be a
big bird, so maybe its wingspan
is as big as an Albatross?

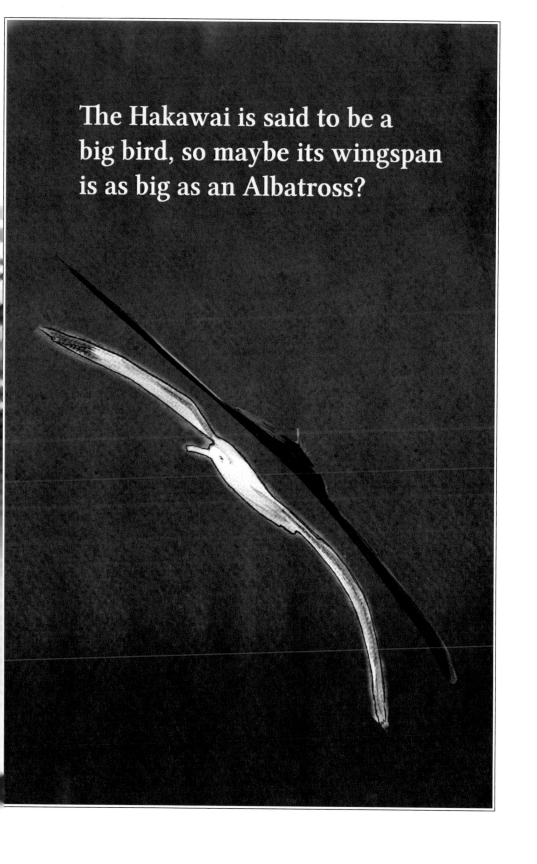

H for Hihi

The Hihi is a cute little New Zealand bird that lives high up in the trees eating nectar. They almost became extinct but were rescued and now you can see them in Wellington's Zealandia reserve.

Twenty six tiny Hihis could
fit on the wings of
an Albatross

I for Ibis

The favourite foods of Ibises
are crayfish and mussels.
In cities they look for food in
rubbish bins so city people
call them 'bin chickens'.

Ibis are about 70 cm long
so four and a half Ibises would fit
along the wings of an Albatross

(Find the half Ibis.)

J for Jabiru

The Jabiru feeds
on fish and shellfish.
It also eats
amphibians like frogs.
The Jabiru catches
its prey by jabbing
it with its large bill.

The Jabiru is a very big bird
with a big wingspan (2.3 m)
but not as wide as the Albatross.

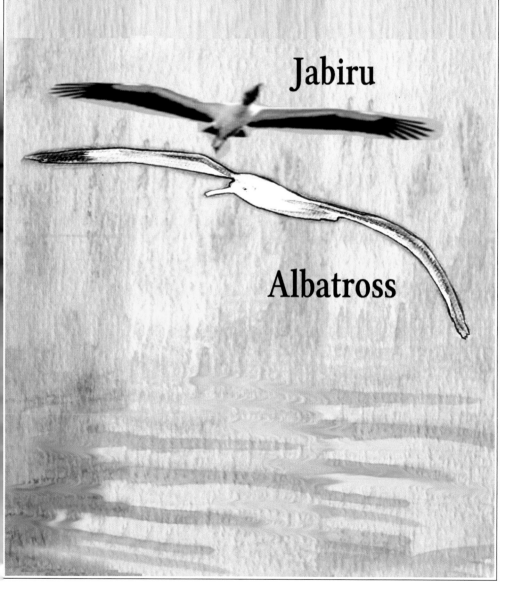

Jabiru

Albatross

K FOR KERERU

(NZ pigeon)

Kereru are usually
silent, though
sometimes they
say a soft 'ooo'.
You can tell if a
Kereru is flying
past even with
your eyes shut
because of its
noisy wing beats.

Seven Kereru would fit
on the wings of an Albatross.

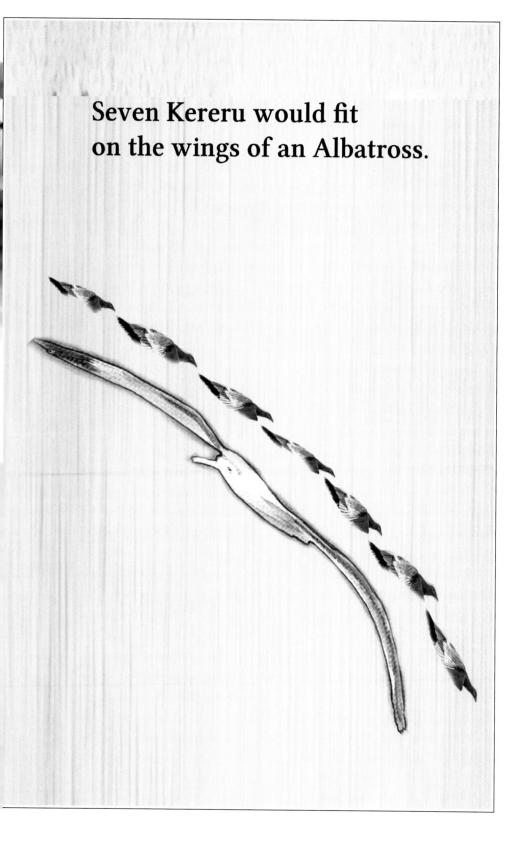

K for Kingfisher

Kingfishers eat mice, frogs and even snakes. Kookaburras are a type of Kingfisher and they sometimes eat venomous snakes which are much longer than they are.

Fifteen Kingfishers could fly
on the wings of an Albatross

K for Kiwi

The Kiwi makes a burrow for its nest. The mother lays a very big egg and the father looks after it.

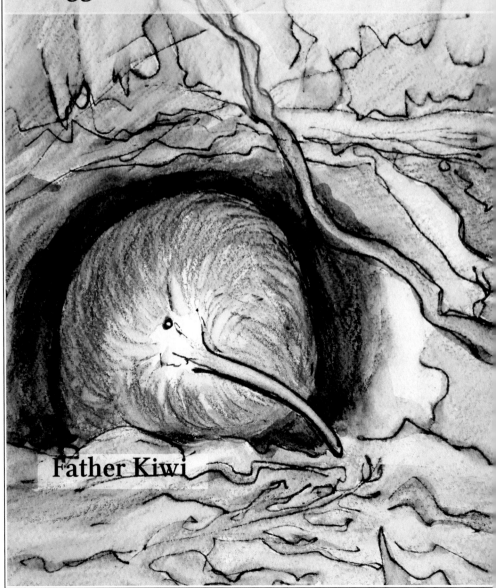

Father Kiwi

Kiwis cant fly. Perhaps they could sit on the back of an Albatross? (There would be room for seven kiwis.)

L for Lorikeet

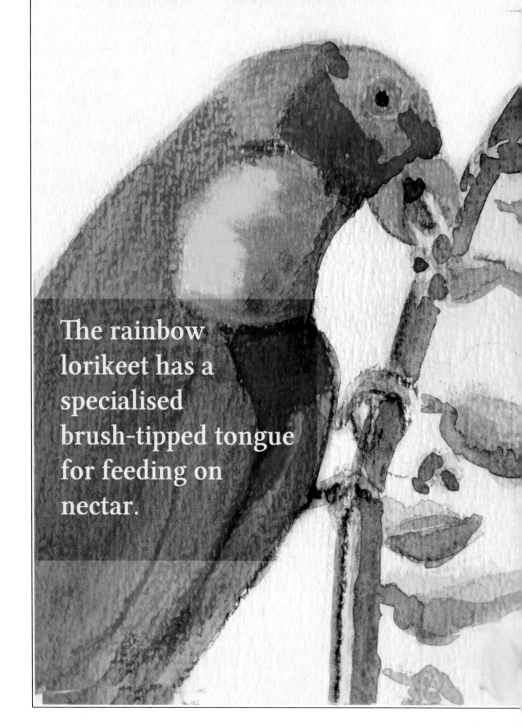

The rainbow lorikeet has a specialised brush-tipped tongue for feeding on nectar.

Lorikeets are about 30cm
long so about eleven would
fit on the wings of
an Albatross.

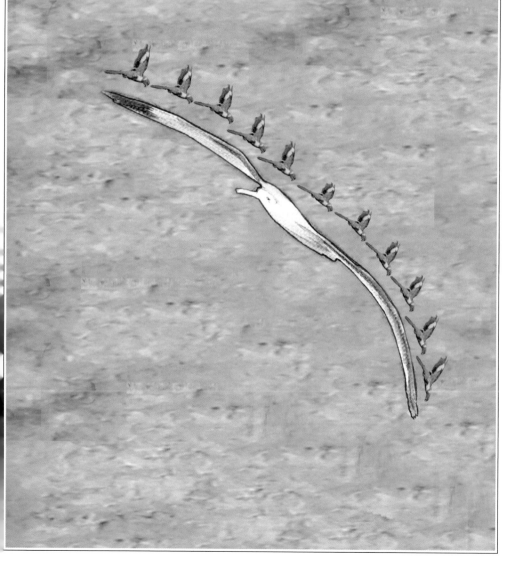

M for Magpie

Magpies, like other birds, sleep
on one leg. One of these magpies
is sleeping and the other is awake.

Eight Magpies could fit on the wings of an Albatross

M for Morepork

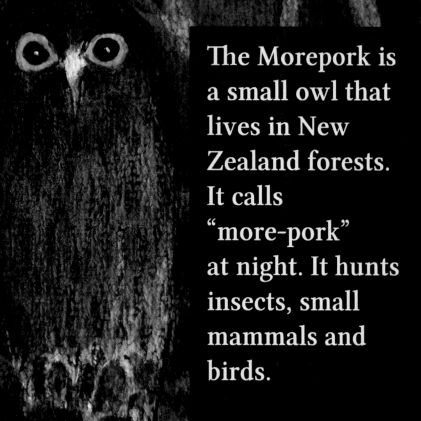

The Morepork is a small owl that lives in New Zealand forests. It calls "more-pork" at night. It hunts insects, small mammals and birds.

The Morepork is almost 30cm tall and twelve Morepork would fit on the wings of an Albatross.

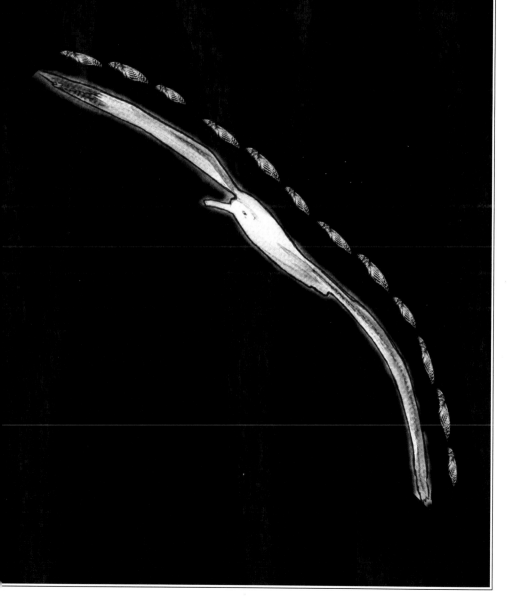

N for Noisy Miner

Noisy miners have a large range of songs, calls, scoldings and alarms. They are gregarious and like living in groups.

Twelve Noisy Miners
would fit on the wings of
an Albatross.

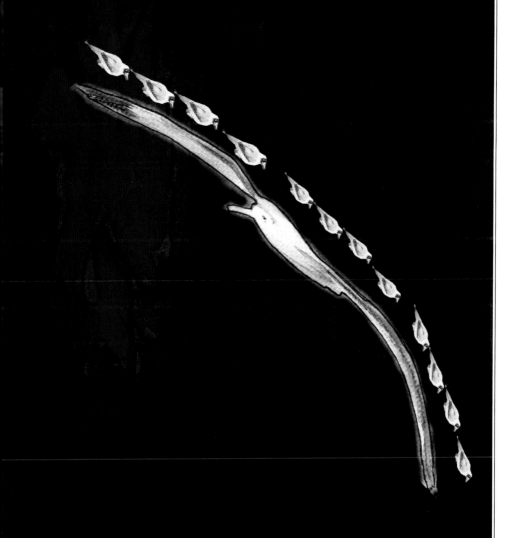

O for Oystercatcher

Oystercatchers
eat shellfish
but also worms,
fish and insect
larvae

Oystercatchers are 50cm
long so seven Oystercatchers
could fit on the back of
an Albatross.

P for Pukeko

Pukeko live in social groups and raise their chicks together.

Seven Pukeko would fit
on the wings of an Albatross.

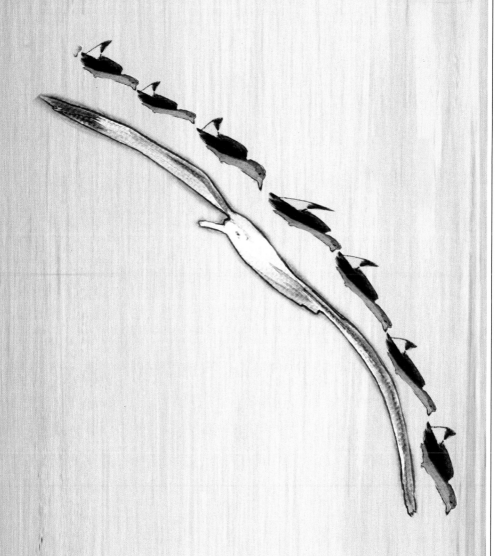

Q for Quailthrush

Quail thrushes hide from danger.
Their mottled coloured feathers
look just like leaf litter and
make them hard to see.

Thirteen Quailthrushes could fit on the wings of an Albatross.

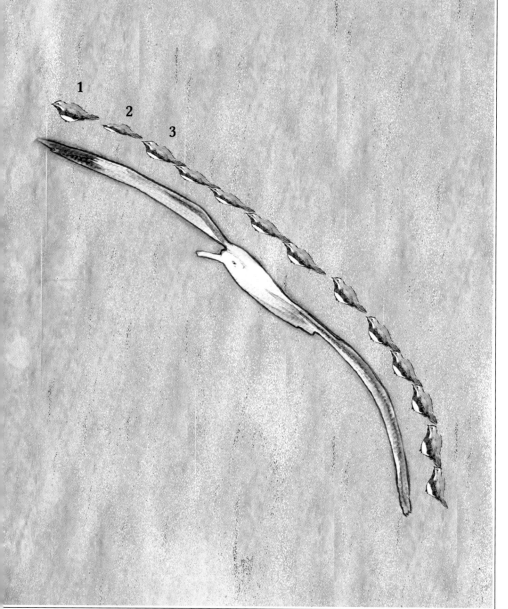

R for Robin

New Zealand Robins are small grey and white birds.

They are friendly and trusting and hop up close to people.

Thirteen New Zealand Robins
could fit on the
back of an Albatross

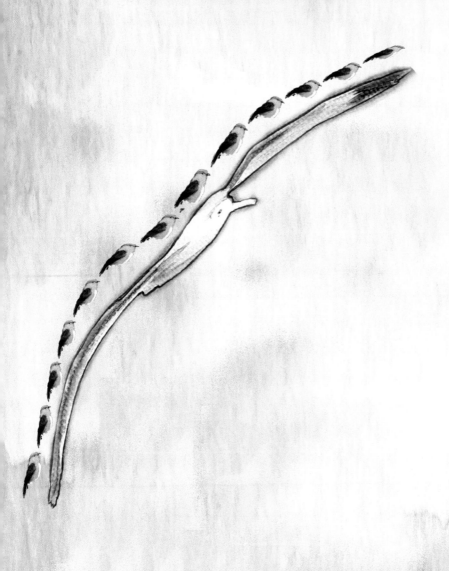

S for Silvereye

The Silvereye is a friendly
forest bird with white rings
around its eyes. Silvereyes
eat insects, fruit and nectar.

Silvereyes are tiny and twenty seven tiny Silvereyes would fit on the back of an Albatross.

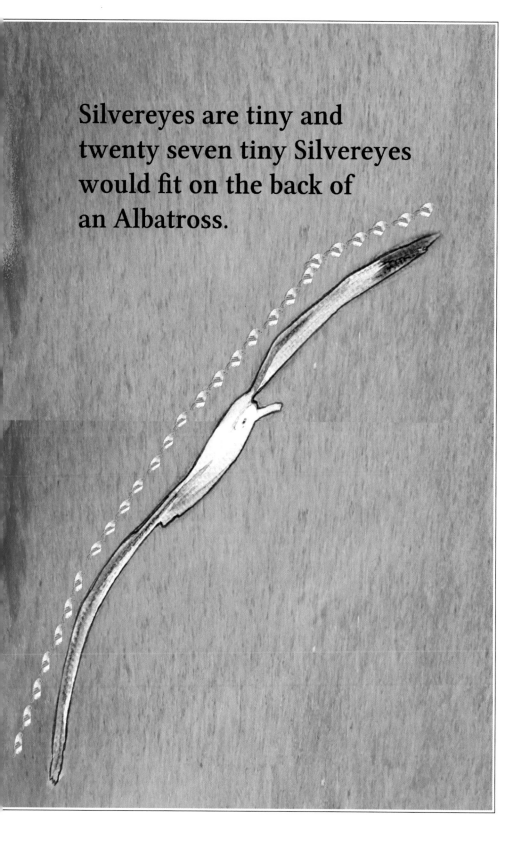

T for Tui

Tuis have white feathers under their throats and feed on nectar. These Tuis are sitting on flax plants

Eleven Tuis could ride on the
back of an Albatross.

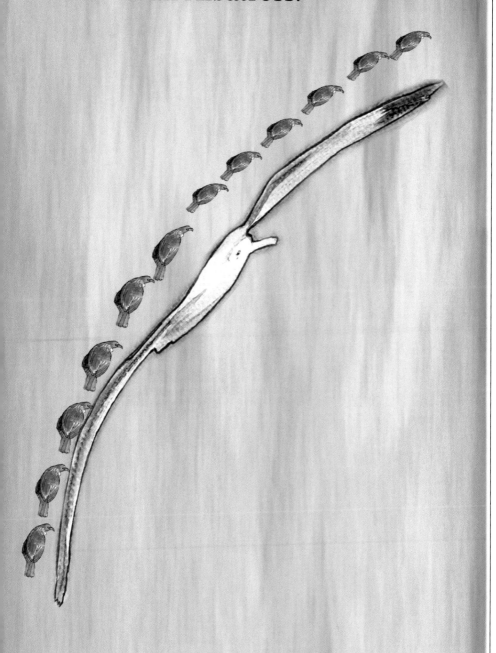

U for Upland Sandpiper

The Sandpiper lives on the
America continent but sometimes
one is seen in
Australia.
They have
very long legs.

Eleven Upland Sandpipers
could ride on the wings
of an Albatross.

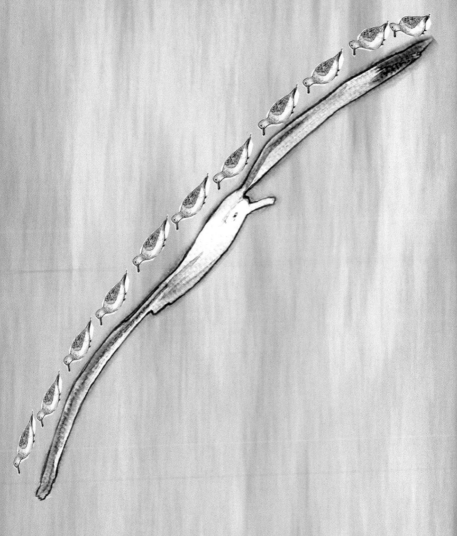

V for Vulture

Vultures are found on every continent except Australia/NZ and Antarctica.

I don't think an Albatross
would want a Vulture riding
on its wings.

W for Weka

Wekas look
like chickens
and eat bugs
and fruit

Wekas are about as big as
chickens and six Weka
could ride on the wings of
an Albatross.

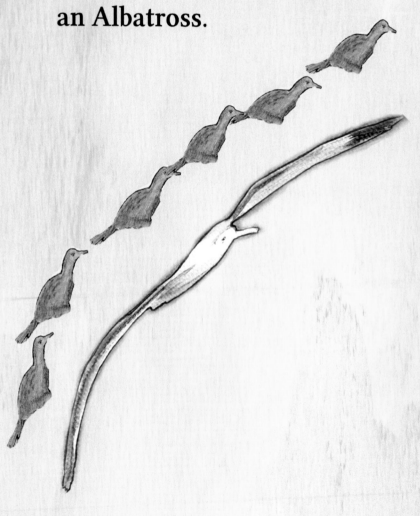

X for Xanthus Hummingbird

Hummingbirds live in
Mexico, not Australia
or New Zealand

Since Hummingbirds
don't live in Australia
or New Zealand
they cant ride on
the back of an Albatross

Y for Yellowhead

The Yellowhead
is also called the
bush canary.
It eats insects.

Twenty three little Yellowheads
could fit on the wings of
an Albatross.

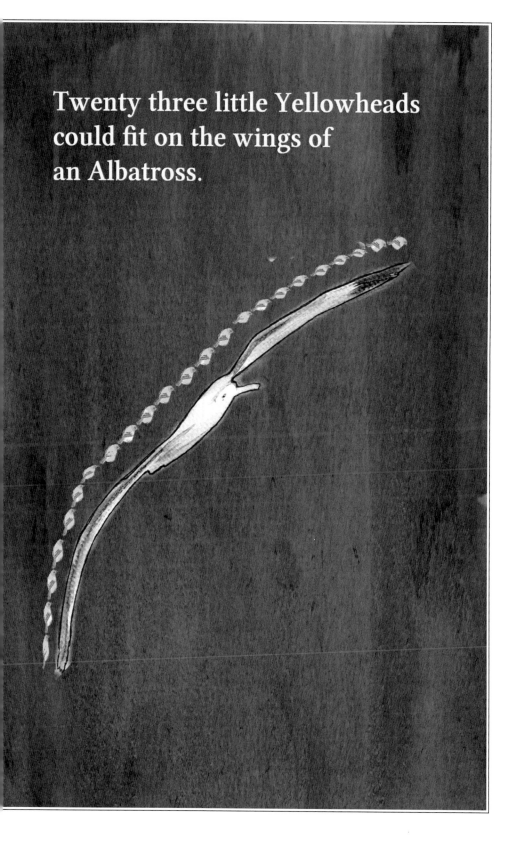

Z for Zebra Finch

The pretty Zebra finch
lives in central
Australia
and is
famous as a
song bird.

The Zebra Finch is a tiny bird
and thirty five could fit
on the wings of an Albatross.